What is Light

Rebecca E. Rehfeld, PhD

Thinking From the Heart
Publications

Thinking From the Heart Publications
A division of TFH™
Minnetonka, Minnesota
Website: www.thinkingfromtheheart.com

First published in the United States of America by Thinking From the Heart
Publications, a division of TFH™ 2008

Copyright © Rebecca E. Rehfeld, 2008
All rights reserved

What is Light

ISBN: 978-0-6152-0326-3 (pbk.)

Printed in the United States of America
Set in Century Gothic

Except in the United States of America, this book is sold subject to the condition that it shall not, by way of trade or otherwise, be lent, resold, hired out, or otherwise circulated without the publisher's prior consent in any form of binding or cover other than that in which it is published and without a similar condition including this condition being imposed on the subsequent purchaser.

The scanning, uploading and distribution of this book via the Internet or via any other means without the permission of the publisher is illegal and punishable by law. Please purchase only authorized electronic editions, and do not participate in or encourage electronic piracy of copyrighted materials. Your support of the author's rights is appreciated.

Cover Art: Digital Expressionism: *Orchid* by Sven Geier
www.sgeier.net

For Thomas, Elizabeth and Guardian

What is Light is a collection of poetry about life, love, spiritual growth, and learning to embrace ourselves as spiritual beings who are currently enjoying a human experience.

Contents

After Eight	84
And Crazy Too	91
As I Am	98
Believing in Magic	97
Bethlehem Night	105
Bloodroot	65
Blowin' Smoke	80
Blue	63
Chant	14
Communion	28
Confessions of the Twelfth Man	107
Daughters and Mothers	94
de Profundus (into the deep)	106
Fade-to-Real	60
Falling Stars	77
Forevermore	30
From the Eaves	62
Fuelling	82
Holy Spirit Come	108
How Many Lives	23
In Season	59
January Thunder	57
Leave-Taking	72
Letting Go	76
Like the Shoulder of a Child	93
Living Inter-dimensionally	36
Lookin' at Me	88
Lovers	83
Love-Speak	81
Mariah Rising	13
Muse	18
New Zealand Crossing, 1899	32
Ole Troubadour	89
One Love	27
raven's Wing	87

River Thief	70
Sinner's Tears	100
Six Times Before	67
Sleepless Night	96
Small Places	16
Spirit Love	24
Still	66
Summer Sprites	38
That Man, Jesus	102
The Child Within	95
Thomas	17
Time	78
Too Young	79
Unborn souls	22
Unwrapped Gift	34
Vagabond Secrets	74
What is Light – Series of Six Poems	
Elizabeth	40
The Unnamed Boy	44
The Father	47
The Mother	49
The Ship's Master	51
John	54
What to Keep	35
When Sarah Plays	26
Where the Wind Blows Wild	92
Windows	25
Winter Fire	29
Winter Grass	90
Winter Leaf	21
Winter Solstice	99
You'd Never Know	86

I dwell in Possibility
A fairer House than Prose
More numerous of windows
Superior – for Doors

Of Chambers as the Cedars
Impregnable of Eye
And for an everlasting roof
The Gambrels of the Sky

Of Visitors – the fairest
For Occupation – this
The spreading wide my narrow hands
To gather Paradise

— Emily Dickinson

What is Light

Mariah Rising

For Phyllis with love

I dreamed they came to me
with clasped hands
circling

Their touch ignited light streams
that arced across time
and domed the earth
in unbounded amnesty

"For you," they said,

Their heart-shaped faces
thrummed healing rhythms
that freed me from the nether
and 50 years of miasmic men —
a lifetime lived
rutting in the roots of trees
trying to drink air
suffocated by dirt

I rose to the ether
like a Phoenix
where we moved effortlessly
through each other
performing pliés
to the faint smell
of cinnamon and myrrh

Chant

He speaks
In a voice six centuries past
and tells me
that in his lifetime
I was low born,
not allowed to speak beyond
a nod or bow.

I served in silence
and helped the braves prepare for hunt
by smoothing warm bear grease
over their bodies
to ease the drag of animal hide against
their warrior backs
and thighs.

When I was old enough
I noticed him —
the tall one
with the thick, black hair women
liked to touch,
and sanded voice
that left us drenched.

In silence, I watched
sun and shadow undulate
against the swell and hollow of his
long body
the way he swayed
when he talked to the wind
canted prayers for rain
and told us of things to come
with his wild drawings of two wolves,
circling

They said he was a soothsayer
living his last life
that he did not eat meat
had never known a woman
and spent his days cross-legged
in prairie grass
keeping vigil

In secret I visited his drawings
again and again
to trace their movements with my fingers
excited by the indomitable spirit of the wolves
until one day he came to me,
both antelope and bear —
graceful, hard

We circled like wolves
until I came alive inside
and began to chant
to feel the ecstasy of my voice
the swell of vibration
and know the thrill of making sound.

Small Places

For Elizabeth with love

The wise woman says sometimes you come to me
as a bird
So I built you a birdhouse.

Centuries ago
you taught me to sing
You, with your throaty smudge
leaving the higher notes to me
like thick, dark coffee and sweet cream
Where grit and the sublime collide.

But in this life you are spirit
You come to me
as a bird
So I built you a birdhouse

Even though my heart knows
none of us is meant to hide
in small places.

Spirit Guide

For Thomas

He waits
among purple iris
and white gardenias
Jesus-like with his
sandaled feet
and red beard

That's how I imagine him
dark nights
when coruscating light
toys with tired eyes
a sense so faithless,
I wonder,
about truth

So what do I trust,
My eyes?
Or the knowing in my heart
that Thomas comes to me,
walking through the purple iris
and white gardenias
talking in a language
calibrated just for us

Muse

For Lee with love

He is an old man
not always able to remember who he was
before.

He knows his bones ache,
the room always feels cold,
and today, there's a dude with wings

hanging out in the corner
that no one else seems to see.
People visit and say things like,

"remember this one, Dad?"
and ask him what he'd like.
All he can think

is that he doesn't like anything
or anyone, except her —
and she never comes

Are they keeping her from him?

Sometimes he can get clear
and remember her bending over him
in the heartbeat of a moment,

before her breath brushes his face,
and he can almost see down the neck
of her dress —

feel the round, softness of her,
lightly kneading his chest.
Makes him rigid, and thankful to God,
all at once

They met during the war.
He was a peace worker,
she was in college.

One dance,
a near kiss that he couldn't forget in seven years.
He saw her again in 1949 when everyone,
determined to forget about the war
was making babies. Lost in her kisses,
and more kisses.

He wasn't her first
but she may as well have been his only.
He loved the way she was without abandon,
the way her breasts swelled in his mouth,
the way she hardly ever put on a robe
to answer the door.

The music came then, hard and fast
as if God had too many things to say
and couldn't pace Himself.
Night after night he tore himself from her
molten
and bent to his music until she came to him

with her soft begging.
They said his music was a "divine gift"
he was "chosen by God"
Things were so good,
but when he asked her to marry him
she slipped away.

Bereft, he thought the music would stop,
but instead had even more to say.
And so he wrote
endlessly
with no sense of time for years, decades —
a lifetime,
accepting commissions and acclaim.

There were times
in any one of the crowds — the crowds all looked the same,
when he thought he saw her.
But it never was,

or maybe it was, he couldn't know for sure
Until one day she was there, unchanged.
"You were always the one," he told her
She nodded gravely, agreeing
"It's the same with me,"
And even before he asked her

to never again leave him
he knew that she would
His music became
Eclectic
disorderly, unpredictable
and still they loved him.

It went on that way —
recognition, success, position
she would appear, just as before.
he can't remember for how long,
or how many times,
or where she is today,
or what today is —

But in those moments when he can get clear
he remembers that all his music,
every note,
even those written before he met her,
wasn't for her, or about her,
or even because of her —

His music *was* her.

Winter Leaf

For Elizabeth with love

I kicked at a winter leaf
as it blew underfoot
It sighed
and skittered on
Like an old soul
free

Unborn Souls

Somewhere she sleeps
in the arms of another
and when she wakes
she plays on the floor
with wooden blocks that stack
and bright plastic donuts that won't

Somewhere my baby munches
on vanilla wafers
and blows soft cookie breath
into the breast of another.

How Many Lives

Sometimes —
when she looks at him
she wonders how many lives
they'll spend together
it hangs in the air, ripe —
like an accidental touch
knowing
    what she can't remember

Sometimes —
she remembers what she can't know
like the feel of coarse muslin
and the weight
of a hand-stitched quilt
the cool heat of a winter fire
    and his clean smile

they were prairie farmers
or migrant workers
she knows
because when his hands fold
soft around hers
    she can feel their labor

Sometimes —
she wonders
if they'll go on this way
stepping through time
together
    until they get it right

Spirit-Love

Like
    reunited
        lovers

they laugh and play

Bending
    slowly
        toward
            each
                other

like a ballet

Until
    they
        touch

and dance

the
    night
        away.

Windows

In the window between ages two and three
he remembered dying —
a free fall from form into light
      no one believed him

At six he remembered art
asking for charcoal instead of crayons
we laughed
      and still didn't believe him

At eight he painted long into the night
until we took away his canvas
and folded up the easel
we tucked him in with a cookie
      and shook our heads at the late hour

In the morning we packed a
peanut butter sandwich
and washed an apple for his lunch,
listening to the wintry song
of a sparrow as it drifted down the
hallway from his room
      we peeked —

And there in the soft light
the boy slept, his left hand tucked neatly
under his cheek
      while the canvas sang

And when he awoke
the window closed.
He asked for his crayons
      and we spoke of it no more

When Sarah Plays

For Sarah with love

If angels were beings
not left to faith,
but seen,

all would know
how they gathered around your head
as you played,
and bent to kiss your hands

how they whispered into your ear,
made sharp your eyes,
and placed their hands gently
leaving their fingerprints
on the keys
with yours.

And when they were filled
they left,
carrying every note
straight into the hearts
of those whom God deemed
needed it most.

One Love

For Trish with love

Before Consciousness
    or air
Before sea cliffs
    or song
Before anything was,
    after every passing —
From one ending
    to the next beginning
there is
    only Love.
One
    Love.

Communion

I closed my eyes to chant-like murmurs
Amorphous sounds, that so often
accompany my sleep
Like parents who talk softly
in an outer room
after their child has been tucked safely in,
and dreamed of her again.

She looked at me with soft eyes
Numinous in knowing
and told me again,
as she has told me before
she didn't leave me,
she never leaves,
she cannot leave.

She holds the container of my life,
reminds me of my purpose
the reason I chose to return,
the life work I have yet to complete —
    Because I can.

Winter Fire

I call your name
At night when I dream
And watch it rise
A flame reaching high

And when I awake
The scent of smoke lingers
As if I never slept
And the dream were true

Night dreams will fade in the play
Of morning light
Yet, still you burn
Like a winter fire

Forevermore

The stars popped as I walked the back roads of
my home town
and came upon the place where the road
rolls into the woods past a small cemetery
few remember —
they are so long ago gone —
when something slipped across the road
in front of me

It looked like a woman fully cloaked
as if to protect herself from the memory
of the boy who made her laugh.
I saw the way the pathless woods
let her pass as if she were their own
and right about then
remembered Olivia's story

Every town has its tale.

On a whim I pushed open the iron gate
to search for the grave of the boy Olivia had loved
it moaned against the movement
and scattered small creatures

The quiet fell still.

As a boy I'd seen the small stone
Scoffed at the faded one-word inscription
that promised one soul to the other
and nearly scoffed again
when I heard a sound soft as air
like the brush of a shoulder against a low-hanging
leaf

I turned and saw the sky part as two owls
rose overhead, streaming north to the stars.

Their calls chorused across the woods and wetlands,
the prairie brushland, and into the town itself
like two souls who have promised
f-o-r-e-v-e-r-m-o-r-e

New Zealand Crossing 1899

(inspired by the film "The Piano")

They say few survived the crossing that year —
Most of them, women.
The handful of men, too sick to do more,
pushed that old piano on to shore
but there was no way to haul it,
    giant thing that it was.

They say it was that last look,
quick and unrepentant, over her shoulder like Lot's wife
as she climbed inland,
    that drove her mad

And there it stood
alone on that barren stretch of beach
swept by the long shadows of afternoon
to be bathed and baked
    by salty turns

They say it's there, still
and times when the east wind
channels through the strings just right
    it blows an eerie, isolated chord

They say, too
that if you watch long enough
you can see sand ghosts
tiptoe across the keys
    until they moan

A few have crossed the beach —
Perhaps it is the legend that draws them,
to place their fingers in the wounds of the scarred, cloudy surface,
see the way it leans,
    and feel each of its long, lonely seasons

They say that when night falls and the moon is high
the tide laps at the piano's ruined wooden legs
and anyone watching knows
what it feels like to be unforgiven
    and to stand alone

Unwrapped Gift

For Victoria with love

She comes to you
faceless,
like an unwrapped gift,
as does most of life —
Something to be named and known
over time.

She hears every softly murmured secret
though she has no ears,
and holds them safely in her heart,
until they are no longer secret
or no longer important.

And when the day comes
That you can see her eyes,
and know the features of her face
as well as your own,
You'll know —

Everyone is an unwrapped gift.

What to Keep

I.

the sun is late
heavy cars grumble
at the morning weight
the road is loud
with gravel, glass
and she twists awake
from her last bad dream

So far
from those other mornings.

II.

What was it
that made her smile
last night before she slept
A feather thought
that tickled
when others would have wept

Now creased by night
into a forgotten wrinkle.

III.

If God
was real
like she wants
to believe
wouldn't nights be deep
with warm
whispered strokes
instead of tangled sheets

And she could choose what to leave behind
and what to keep.

Living Inter-dimensionally

I dreamt I was hanging outside the window
of a 70-story building on a trapeze,
trying to control so many things
from this untenable place.

Inside, my trusted servant reached through the window
to hand me everything I asked for.
And, each time I took it,
my hold on the trapeze became more tenuous.

I was flirting with falling —
my fingers so full, they hurt.
The back of my knees cinched the narrow bar,
slipping.

But like a reflex
I kept reaching out and taking,
So I fell.

At first my fall was meteoric.
There were others falling, too
some faster than others
each clutched armfuls of coveted wealth
terror etched on their faces.

Wildly I thought, it's all these things
They're making me fall faster
I have to let go—
They are my death.

The centrifugal force made it difficult to
loosen my fists — open my fingers
to release all the things I held so tightly
but I fought for freedom

As my fingers opened
all the things sprang free
and my fall slowed.

How easily now I floated
And, free of fear
grew softer, lighter
until my feet connected with the earth
without impact.

Safe on the ground
It all looked the same,
but I felt different.
So different, that I looked for myself

and couldn't find me
anywhere
Because I was everywhere
and nowhere

I was light and air
I was hope and love
I was everyone.

Summer Sprites

Night falls,
summer night
when the last red streaks leave the sky
Gaia opens to ether
what she cannot hold

You and I, summer sprites
stroke the sea, skim the sky,
like twin tides in twirl
unbounded,
these sweet summer nights

And at autumn's eve
you take my hand
mortal again
Every season ends.

What is Light

A series of six poems inspired by the life of Elizabeth Tilley Howland 1607-1680, a Mayflower traveler, pilgrim, and survivor. While the characters and *some* of the events are real, the poetry is a fictional description intended to emphasize that life without light is not tolerable, in any century, for any reason.

I. What is Light — Elizabeth

Even now
I cannot speak his name,
that boy,
so sweet with intention,
he could not bear it when I removed
my coif to free my hair,
and placed his soft hand against my breast.

I cannot speak of my boldness
because I fear one day we may be in the
annals of this new world —
for surely they will write of this barren, empty land we call
Plymouth Rock.
Aptly named,
so thoroughly has she rejected us
she would spit us back into the Atlantic
if she could.

Will they romanticize
and use words like "courageous?"
Or, will they recognize it for what it was
A people who,
forced to set aside their beliefs,
chose uncertainty and death —
and found both.

Even now
when I close my eyes
I am 15 again,
in high winds riding the waves,
my body balances easily with the pitch and toss of the
ship,
intoxicated by the way she toys with us —
She could take us at any time.

And my Father,
so weak he can hardly stand straight,
wonders if it was folly,

and worries so about Mother —
I am invisible.

The boy,
unable to tolerate sea life
hides in the bilge
and lays his head in my lap
face down after being sick
consumed by shame.

I stroke his hair and allow my fingers to trace
his profile,
the softness of his wide lips,
feel the drag of his young beard
and the wilted lace at his collar,
then slip my hand under his doublet.
But he groans and turns away.

"it's alright. Only one of us needs to be strong," I whisper.

Sometimes, even I am afraid of my strength.

We have been on the Mayflower for nearly two months,
and what began as low whispers in the early days
has grown to strident disagreement,
even accusation.
Some want to turn back.
Others are certain we're lost.
And still others hold fast.

I have to watch the dogs
They will steal my mother's food
if I turn away for even a moment.

And last night, a handful of men met with my father
in secret
asking him to take over.
I was fiercely proud,
But surprised when my father declined
and instead spoke of prayer, community and purpose.

The men became angry and for days after
sent dark looks our way.

Even now
I can see the way the land looked in those snowy
November moments before the morning light;
purple, gray, brown —
colors I hadn't seen on the horizon for months.
I called for my father, my mother,
I wanted to call for the boy
but instead called for the Ship's Master.

Suddenly everyone was on deck;
even the sick,
straining to believe what they saw.
Father died within the year,
didn't live long enough to plant even one crop.
Mother followed him a month later.
They shuffled me to the Carvers,
who died trying to plant their first field,
and I was left to wonder about a God
who would crush good people.

I had just turned 16
when John found me in the high heat of day,
alone on that rocky sliver of land,
working the plow against an unrelenting earth
that now held so many of us,
my Father, my Mother,
the Carvers,
perhaps even the boy —
I couldn't know.

Even now
I remember the way he rode up fast,
the way he reined his horse up short,
the way his eyes widened as he took in
my unrestrained hair
naked arms
and open bodice,
the flex of my muscles

I remember the way he slid easily from the beast's back
and knelt to take the earth in his fingers.
I turned away to smooth my hair,
to pull my clothing,
and my senses,
together —
and when I turned back
for the first time, I understood
how a burden
can become light.

II. What is Light — The Unnamed Boy

I dare not speak the name
of that red-haired aristocrat —
the girl, whose father seeks peace, still.
Day after day on this wretched boat
we watch our dignity unravel
The men seem smaller
The women harder
and the children always hungry
One was nearly swept overboard today
and I was unable to do more than call out.

I dare not speak her name
because one day when this is over
and we are there,
or dead,
someone, somewhere will write about it
And I could not bear for people to know
how much I admired her strength,
the way she cared for her mother, believed in her father,
danced wild with the wind,
and ran barefoot across the flat planks until it grew too cold,
often showing me more than her toes.
No, I could not bear for anyone to know
That, at 17, I could not match her strength
or return her love.

It was forbidden to be on deck in a storm
yet one mid-October gale several weeks into
the voyage, we stole above.
Rain had just begun to fall
and the ragged wind tore at everything.
I begged her to let us return below
but she laughed and pulled at one of the ties of her coif
letting the wind do the rest
It was a brazen move.

Her red hair splayed against her shoulders
and down her back
She turned to me, then
and began to loosen her bodice
until the wind blew her naked

She laughed and caressed herself
then swept her arms wide, and invited me closer.
When I didn't move
she took my hands
and placed them against her bare breasts

I wanted to feel something, to be excited,
but the roll of the waves was too much,
and I turned away, sick

I fled to the darkest corner of the bilge
where it stank so badly
no one could tolerate it

Perhaps it was shock —
What man expects a girl
a *good* girl
to strip in a storm,
on an over-crowded ship
where anyone might see?
I reached down and groped my length,
thinking to punish myself for not wanting her
and was surprised when the hardness came

She found me in this state
and drew me to her lap
where I hid my face for long moments

This woman-child
whose name I dare not say
began to trace the length of my face
down my throat,
under my doublet and trousers
and because I was still hard, I let her

But her touch was distracting and in a moment
I was no longer a man
I pushed her hand aside and turned to the wall

"It's alright," she whispered
"Only one of us needs to be strong."

III. What is Light — The Father

I am a man of peace!
What do they want from me?

We are all of us
hungry
and cold!
So many are sick,
the relentless rocking curdles our stomachs
and the wind never ceases.

At night, it sounds like the wail of a lost soul
denied heaven
and unwilling to enter hell.

A handful of men —
good men
hardened by fear,
came in secret a fortnight ago to tell me
the firewood has grown dangerously low.
Soon, we'll have to spend what little strength we have, to
tear apart the ship.
Already we have begun to tear at each other.
And that fool for a ship's master,
they think he may not even know where we are.

But I am a man of peace!
Why do they turn to me?

They spoke of overthrowing the council —
How could I sanction premeditated betrayal?
For the first time, I realized how easy it is
to hold moral ground
to be just
to follow God's commandments
when the bellies of men are full
and their women, contented.

When I think of the choices I have already made
just to survive —

And my daughter,
this is no place for her.
There is not even a small corner
to preserve a modicum of privacy
she has seen too much.

After the men left
she looked at me with eyes that held no light
She does not yet know,
that the true measure of a man is defined as much
by his choices
as by his actions —
and that "no" can be as courageous as "yes"

I hope, at least, to teach her this.

IV. What is Light — The Mother

I am dying
My husband knows
but will not accept it,
and my daughter *cannot* know

She is so fierce —
the youngest and most brave
of all our children.
The light of curiosity burns within,
and we have taught her to believe she can
accomplish anything.

She will be the only one of us who survives this.
I know,
because
although he tries to hide it
my husband is failing, too.
I see the way he can no longer stand straight
The way he gives us most of his daily rations.
How will he build our farm in the new land?

My sister and her husband
have come on this wretched voyage, too.
They are wild-eyed with fear
A few weeks ago, their little boy was almost swept
overboard
It was that lusty young man, John
who saved the child.
We don't see much of him
I can't imagine where he keeps himself
on this ship where there is no such thing
as privacy.

They tell me he is a hired man, the youngest son
born to a gentleman farmer, and thus, no inheritance.
He will be free when we reach the new land.
I can't help but wish my daughter had been on deck
to see him rescue the boy

Even in my old age and poor health
the sight of him
as the light played against his muscular frame
made me catch my breath.
But she was below deck, sorting rations
and keeping the dogs at bay.

If I had even a moment's doubt about
the likelihood of my recovery
it was dashed today when we saw the new world
on the horizon.

Even the knowledge that we had
ridden the relentless Atlantic, and won
could not release me from the grip of melancholy
or tamp the incessant cough,
or clot the blood.

V. What is Light — The Ship's Master

August 1, 1620:
The *Mayflower* and the *Speedwell*
have been commissioned at last!
100 people,
Separatists who suffer religious persecution,
And Strangers, who hold no particular religious loyalty
have elected to cross the Atlantic —
to settle in Jamestown on the Hudson —
to begin again in a new land.
I, Christopher Jones, am the Ship's Master.

September 6, 1620
The *Speedwell* has sprung a leak;
It is patched,
but we may have to turn back.

September 10, 1620
The *Speedwell* has sprung another leak
and is unseaworthy
I saw the disappointment on their faces
but they did not hesitate.
We are all to cross on the *Mayflower*.

September 12, 1620
The *Mayflower* is a sweet ship
Year-over-year, leakage from the wine casks,
has neutralized the garbage and other filth
thrown into the hold by sailors too lazy
to hoist it overboard
Disease should not be a problem on this voyage.

September 16, 1620:
After some delay, we have weighed anchor
We are now, all 100 of us on the *Mayflower*
It is difficult
These people are not used to such a lack of privacy
Uneasy on my mind is that sabotage of the *Speedwell*
is suspected

September 21, 1620:
This is the last time I will agree
To make this voyage
The Atlantic, always treacherous
Is wretched this time of year
Five days out and already I see signs of dissension
among the ranks, and the passengers

September 27, 1620:
I have heard quiet grumblings among the men
They think we are lost
I have shown them time and again
the light in the night sky
and explained which stars are used
to navigate

October 2, 1620:
It grows worse
I had to give one of the men,
loud with baseless accusation,
a thorough drubbing
Morale is dangerously low.

October 16, 1620:
These foolish, foolish people!
Today we almost lost a child
A *child*!
because of carelessness
If it hadn't been for my hired man, John,
the child would surely have drowned

October 23, 1620:
I know they are plotting
One of the council leaders came to warn me
of a possible mutiny.
Worse, today, I was able to confirm what I have
suspected for some time —
The inclement weather has forced us off course
How far, I cannot say.

November 1, 1620:
Time grows long
Almost everyone is either sick
Or weary
Or both
And I am nearly undone
The skies are unyielding
unreadable
and the ship's compass has been destroyed
by the constant damp

November 9, 1620
Today, after 65 days at sea, we heard a joyful cry
It was the girl,
the spirited one with the red hair who saw it first — land!
There, in the morning light,
land became visible on the horizon
As if waking from the dead,
men and women crawled from below,
to see what the light had brought.

November 11, 1620
At last, we have reached land
We were blown off course so often,
it will take some time to determine where we are
This is not the rich land of the Hudson
All the same, thanks be to God Almighty
who has led us to the shores
of a new land.

VI. What is Light — John

The first time I saw her she was fending off the dogs,
who were docile enough during the day
but at night, formed a pack to catch rats
and anything else they could find.
Food left for her sick mother
was an easy target.

She was magnificent
and sent the dogs howling as they scattered.
I made her out to be about 16,
a girl, really, not yet quite a woman.
I learned her name much later — Elizabeth;
I don't think she saw me at all.

The next time I saw her
she and that boy were sneaking
up to the deck in the early moments
of a storm.
I followed, intending to warn them
but became transfixed
as the wind sent her white coif flying overboard.

I watched her laugh and tease the boy
more playful than lusty.

She reached up and loosened her hair.
It rained red down her back, past her hips
and whipped sideways into the wind.

I tried again to warn them
but my warning stopped short in my throat
when she began to loosen the ties of her bodice
until the wind blew her naked to the waist.
She raised her head
and danced across the deck letting the rain bathe
her bare
It was all I could do to keep my balance

When lightening flashed, the boy turned
and ran away
retching as he went
Poor kid just couldn't get his sea legs.

She never knew that I saw them that day
She left soon after the boy, taking the back way
down to the bilge.

Afterward,
I could not get her out of my head
— forget what I'd seen in that dark devil of a storm

A few days later, land was spotted on the horizon
and the real work began.
We were thankful to be done with the sea
but it was a desolate land,
No homes, or fires, or food awaited us.
Only an unrelenting wind,
and winter, colder than we'd ever known.

When the common buildings had been
thatched together,
acreage agreed upon,
and a few homes fashioned,
only 49 of us remained
to begin our first season of planting.
Scurvy and pneumonia had claimed 51 lives
But spring had come
And the promise of light-filled days
was upon us.

By now,
Elizabeth was orphaned
and living with the Carvers
until one day in late May
we learned there had been a farm accident
and only Elizabeth survived

When the news came that she was
working the land alone

I could stay away no longer
she was only 16,
I hoped it was old enough

I'd never been to the Carvers' land
Came upon it faster than intended
and had to rein my horse up short
She was in the field working
sweat trickled down the open bodice
between her breasts
her tanned arms were bare and flexed against the plow

Her eyes widened as I slid out of the saddle
And when I bent to touch the earth
it was because I was surprised to find
that she had already plowed most of the field

She turned away from me
and I saw her smooth her hair
the way a woman will,
and when she turned back
there was warmth in her eyes

"It's you," she said
And in that light-filled moment
I understood
the girl had become a woman.

January Thunder

The first time I watched him,
my fire, nothing but a few embers,
I thought he was a night wanderer,
but soon realized
it is morning that calls him —
    like me

In the least-known hours of morning
He slips from his bed, blows on his hands
and heads out across the lake past my cabin
pulling a loaded sled over snow skiffs
until in the still-dark, his feet find the spot —
as if they can feel the fish pulse below.

It's a big lake,
and slow to freeze each year
until it is some time in January
before the layers become one.

And so I began to listen for the sound of his boots
and the scrape of his sled,
to watch the ritual of ice, man, and element,
until I could anticipate just when he'd turn
his head away from the wind
to check his lines,
    always two lines.

The first time I heard it
I thought it was thunder,
or men working on the railroad tracks
some far distance away
and wondered what drives men to do that
kind of work in the dark,

And then one morning, he didn't come
A blue-gray dawn rose, heavy and still
I waited —
Long after I'd crawled back into the ticking

I heard his soft whooshes and hard thuds
pass over the walkway of my cabin.

He'd never come in the light.
Before I knew what I was doing
I had warmed a thermos for coffee and added
a touch of chocolate

My own boots were loud
and scuffed the snow, like a true tenderfoot.
There was no surprise on his face
when I knelt on the ice beside him,
    his mustache stiff with frost.

He nodded as I uncapped the thermos
taking the coffee I offered
and keeping the silence
as if he knew
morning is no time for questions

Only the sound of ice splitting
across the far side of the lake
where the north wind and weak sun
negotiate a tentative armistice
    sounding like January thunder.

In Season

The birds don't come on windy days
they're grounded by gale-busters
in late November
that rip
at rusted winter oak leaves
and clot the feeders

The jack rabbits
tunnel under tree roots,
and ducks
exiled
by indurate ice
hide in the brush.

But the deer remain.
They come in threes and fours
to munch on the sweet wild growth
that springs from ice-covered quicksand,
and is only in season
November through March.

Fade-to-Real

the clouds looked pregnant, and the air turned
suddenly fetid the way it gets on a hot day
when the climate is so stressed,
only an explosion of rain can wash it calm.

I was anxious to be home,
before the dirt path became sloppy — to stay dry.
My dog was jumpy —
He's always jumpy, but the low rumbles made his
hindquarters twitch, and he pulled hard at the leash.
Nearly a mile left to go, I thought,
just as the first drop splashed against the toe of my
shoe.

That's when I saw her.
She stood like statuary —
so still, she was difficult to discern from the rest of
nature
but for the white flip of her tail.

The rain backed off, then
as if it didn't want to get us wet
the doe, my dog... me.

She was beautiful.
Gangly yet graceful; timid yet serene
So natural in her element.
I just wanted to look at her
and thank her for being in the meadow with me
So I whispered softly, You take my breath away

She moved her head then,
and the meadow awoke with soft movement
as a dozen deer came into view.

They had been there all along as grass, trees, bark, even earth,
Shape shifters who would not be seen until they chose it.

They took their time as they crossed the path,
hooves lightly scudding against gravel and dirt.
Occasionally one would cast a look of near-concern
not so much at me as at my dog.

My heart quickened as I watched each one fade
back into tree and bush, back into bark and earth,
without brushing a branch or flattening a blade of grass,
until they slipped into the cover of thicket.

From the Eaves

Some winters
like men,
are harder than others.
You can tell
by the Bastille-like
stalactites —

Daggers that hang heavy
from the eaves
like frozen bruises
that won't go away
until the spring melt,

And even then
may leave a few scars

Calyx

Long
have I slept
  a bud
Waiting
for the Light to
  unfurl my
soul

Blue

One morning
I awoke to a behemothic
blue bed
My husband went to work
without a word
never even glanced my way

The maid came and
made the bed with me in it —
just went about her business despite my
silent
protests,
the chippie

as if I she couldn't see me
among the 800 thread count
and square folds —
smaller than a speck
speckless

When she came to strip the bed
on laundry day
I was balled up, tossed down the chute
and promptly buried under
my husband's boxers
and other soiled discards

I should have been worried about
time in the washer
but in order to worry
there must be expectation
So easy to be
a speck

The spin cycle gave me a little trouble
Still, I felt almost cogent
when I emerged
so I tried to think of the dryer

as a vacation somewhere
in the southwest

But I was
just a speck
that might blow away like top soil
at any moment
and become lost with the other specks

Bloodroot

Brittle world
like standing a puzzle on end
to watch the white-on-white
pieces fall, clueless
cue-less as the bloodroot
whose white petals
hide treacherous roots
that bleed beneath the surface
Blunt aspiration.

Still

When the owl called long
after midnight
my cat went for cover
and I knew to listen for secrets —
    watch for you

She said you would crawl like night
into my dreams
melt 20 years in a moment with your
faded eyes and incarnadine fire
that hold no heat
or heart
    still

Six Times Before

Sure, it's late
but the kids need milk for morning
and she'll want coffee
She adjusts the bag between her hip and
the crook of her arm
and pushes out the supermarket door
into the dark

"Hey, Baby"
She hears his gritty whisper

"Did you think you could get away?"
She smells sour liquor

"That's right, Baby, it's me. An' you ain't
been so good to your old man, lately"

His voice scratches as he circles into view
runs his big-knuckled fingers over her lips —
lips still bruised from the last time.

"You owe me," he scrapes, his arm like an
iron snare, forces her neck so she has to
look at him square in the eyes —
eyes that burn hot
Hard
Like the feel of his fist when it slams into
her jaw

She tries to keep a blank face
That's one of the rules, she remembers
but her eyes flick toward her car

"Now, Baby, don't make me lose my
patience," he warns
"Don't make me hurt you — you know I

don't want to, but Babe, you make me
do it when you run away like this.
Ain't you left me 'bout six times before?
An' ain't I always taking you back?

Say, how you gonna buy them pretty high
Heels you like so much if you're on your own,
hmmm?

An' just what," he says, dragging his fat tongue
across her cheek, "are you gonna do
without my long hard body to squeeze?

That's right, Baby, you can't get away
from me — I'm everywhere."

She hears him suck in his breath
and the wet, loud sound his tongue makes
as he pushes it in and out of her ear.

She stops struggling, feels her body grow still

"That's right, Baby, don't fight it," he says,
between flicks
his hands grasp her thick hair,
drag her face into his mouth

She never sees the milk explode across asphalt
or the can of coffee roll into the mud.

As people begin to gather in the street,
she rocks back and forth over his fallen body,
fingers convulsing around the gun
expecting him to lunge

But for the first time
he looks small.
And when she finally notices the spilled milk
trickling across tar
She feels the loosening ache of a single tear

River Thief

I guess it was the day little Bobby Fisher's red trike
floated by — without Bobby
that I knew my Daddy wasn't comin' back,
either.

We was standin' knee-deep near the edge
diggin' for drifters when Bobby's Mama saw it
She just crumpled into the water after it,
holdin' out her hand, like the river was gonna
give somethin' back

Nights, we slept in the church
rolled up in musty old blankets donated by them
mission women tryin' to keep warm.
My sister, Carrie, would cry —
Mostly she said I was holdin' her hand too tight

Our Daddy used to say
'memberin' somethin' good
made the bad times easier
so I kept thinkin' about that one date I'd had
with Bobby Fisher's brother, Nate
an' the way his sweet mouth tasted
in the dark

it made the hard church floor fall away
and the stars come out of their hiding places,
the wind blew a little softer through the splintered glass
an' I didn't wish so bad for a pillow

When the river went away
it seemed like we didn't have nothin' left
that wasn't wet'
or rusted
or broke
An' even thinkin' about Nate
couldn't stop me from wonderin'
why —

Leave-Taking

Each night for four nights before
Daniel Thomas missed the curve
he dreamed --
the dreams followed him long into day.

In the first dream, he saw
Archangel Michael
guide the safe landing of every airplane
coming into Detroit.
Daniel Thomas had never been to Detroit,
rarely traveled,
didn't usually remember dreams,
and was vaguely irritated when the
dream came back to him
over his morning coffee,
his drive to work,

his mid-morning meeting with Finance,
lunch with a sales rep from Moline,
and was still with him
on his drive home that evening.

On the second night, he dreamed of
Elijah scaling the clouds in his
incarnadine chariot.
Daniel Thomas hadn't read the
Old Testament in years,
didn't usually remember dreams,
and got to thinking of one or two
other stories he'd learned as a child.

On the third night, he watched as he
kissed his wife a tearful goodbye, and
contemplated the empty suitcase
spread open across the bed.

No matter how hard he tried, he
couldn't think what to pack.
In the morning, he wondered where
his wife had stored their suitcases,
and considered the possibility
of a vacation.

On the fourth night he dreamed of
his older brother Brian, who was lost
in the tangles of Viet Nam in 1972,
and never found.
No words passed between them as
they tossed back beers for the first time,
bathed in his brother's refulgent smile.

On the fifth day when Daniel Thomas
missed the curve
he floated like Elijah in a chariot
guided by Archangel Michael,
saw his sleeping wife, who was not yet
aware of his sudden departure,
and understood why the suitcase
had been empty.

He would need nothing, now --
Nothing but to take Brian's outstretched hand
so as not to miss this next curve.

Vagabond Secrets

I.
She puts away her thumb, sunburned from hitchhiking when an old Volkswagen van skids to the shoulder. "Got a long ways to go?" She likes his voice and the way he wears his Dodgers cap low, and the way she sinks into the velour of the van, even better. She sleeps to the slow reassuring VW chug, letting the highway transform both the immediate, and the future, into past.

II.
They have breakfast in LaJara where the air is flat. Dusty. Sad. He orders hot water for his thermos and in a quiet voice, talks about his boy back home. Lunch is in Taos at one of those outdoor cafes strung with colored lights and hand-made wind chimes made by Hispanic immigrants with no green card. He orders more hot water and buys a brightly colored piñata for his boy, he explains, in that same quiet voice. Then pulls the bill of his Dodgers cap lower.

III.
Dinner is a snack somewhere along the interstate. He shares his private stock of peanut butter crackers and green tea. His fingers expertly pinch the tea from the bag. Slightly bitter, it swells warm in her belly while the night air cools.

IV.
Long after dark, he pulls to the shoulder. She sees the way tears have collected on his eyelashes and in the grooves of his face. "You drive," he says. She takes the wheel and waits. Every highway vagabond has a secret, she knows.

V.
Dark air wraps around his words threading each syllable with meaning. The piñata, he says, will never belong to his

boy. "Leukemia." He lets out his breath in spare measures. "One day the boy was just too tired."

VI.

He sleeps while she drives, listening to his snoring, light, like the quiet of his voice. Rain collects on the windshield in wet, dotted explosions. She slides her right hand along the dash for the wiper. It feels dusty and flat — flat like the table in Taos. Dusty, like the LaJaran streets. And sad — like a child's piñata that will never see a child.

Letting Go

There was a faucet
in the back yard
    which hadn't been used
      for years

And feeling the need
 to clean up
    she opened that
      faucet

Water gushed
   through those rusty pipes
      tearing at bits
         of corroded metal,
            bumping and scraping
as they were forced along,
  and she heard the pipes
     scream in anguish
         as they tried to expand
            under the pressure

Until finally,
 all the bits of spoiled metal
     and rusty liquid
       were expelled

Leaving only
 clean,
    clear,
      water

Falling Stars

The glacier creeps
in silence —
fills her throat
Thick
until her music is smothered
Thin
as a dying baby's cry
and notes stray off the staff
      lost

Falling stars, they say
are old
They spoil and drop
out of orbit in a brief,
silent, flare
But she thinks, perhaps
They simply grew too cold —

And in the silence
they become nothing

Time

For Elizabeth

The last time I saw you
your smile had just a trace
    of sadness

There were so many things
    left undone
and words
    left unspoken

But you knew
    and so did I
    that it was time

Good-bye, friend

You could be sleeping late
    or off on a trip somewhere
and that's why you don't
    answer the phone

But last night, I dreamed about
    a candle
and when I went to put out the flame
    it flickered stubbornly,
then seemed to go out by itself
    the smoke kept rising,
until it reached an open skylight,
    then passed out of sight

And that was you, wasn't it

Too Young

When she passed,
before Spirit and Soul united
she watched her mother weep
   — inconsolable
saw the mute bend of her father
and felt the sorrow of centuries
settle heavy in their hearts
like sediment
that won't be swept clean
in this lifetime

Blowin' Smoke

Them old flames
lickin' at me again
like some kind of spirit

I keep waitin'
Figure they just gonna burn
'til they can't no more
burnin' on plenty
of fresh tinder
'cause my heart is so smoky, maybe
from the slow sounds
I keep thinkin' we'd make
Like the crazy wail
of a saxophone
just because the man
curls his lips
an' blows

Smokin'
an' hot

The kind iced lemonade won't cool
deep in the dog days of August
an' you

All sultry
an' ready
an' me

… burnin'

Lovespeak

Energy
designed to wound
or warm
to wind around hidden curves
and wander into private moments
To palliate or promise

They are mistrals that shift the heart
and leave us windswept —
waiting

Let me step into
the wilds of your words
wear them like lingerie
exquisite, reckless

Let me roll in them
molten
until they are no more
until we rise
in rapture

Fuelling

A capricious summer wind
squeezes zigs of rain
through the pumping screen
where two bodies, frescoed and
folded into the softest
of hiplocks
ride the long glide,
and burble monosyllabic
moans

— the coffee waits

Lovers

The
dripping
wax
of the candle
molds
like a lover
to the stem

Embracing
the
night
long after the flame
has
cooled

After Eight

She's been gone a long time, now
Yet I remember that airless, glassy
summer when I was 12 —

Every time I turned a corner
they'd be whispering, wearing mean looks,
    the old hens
'til finally when winter came,
 she up and left
 sayin' it was just too damn cold!

I saw her once
standing at the edge of a jagged sea drop
letting the wind tangle her hair
and catch at the slender length of green
she wore around her neck
until unwound,
the freed thing lifted and floated over the edge

She was laughing that day
so much, her shoulders trembled
until the strap of her dress
slid off the slope of her shoulder
    naked

After awhile
most everyone forgot.
I guess a good story can sure grow stale quick.
But even though I was only a boy of 12
I knew what had them all a-buzz.

She had this smile,
teasing-like
the kind you put on for a man
after eight in the evening
when moments are opaque
and morning
    is a lifetime away

You'd Never Know

If I left now,
I'd wander around,
    searching

For eyes that say the things,
and lips that smile the way
    yours do

And you'd never know
just how much I was still
    with you

raven's wing

the lonely sound
of a train car
rattlin' as it rounds the tracks
going somewheres so fast
he cain't even see where he is
less'n someone pulls the brake line

that'd do it —
pull the brake line
an' take a look at the tall grass blowin'
an' the sky all big and full
an' the sun
all hot on those rocks

and that raven haired gal over there,
smilin'
and flushed;
like she'd like to dance with me
and twirl
'til there's just one of us
Flying

Lookin' at Me

Hey now,
Who's that boy lookin' at me, so fine
sittin' at the bar with biker's arms
and blue eyes that know

Hey now,
Just who is that boy with his left shoulder slumped
like he's gonna dive into me
and his Levis worn just right

And, what would it be like
to hear him whisper without movin' his lips
tellin' me things he ain't told no one
Sayin' Hey now, girl
Let's go!

Ole Troubadour

There he goes again
chasin' after every damn thing
the fool,
Like we don't already have enough trouble!
Some people just got too much air.

He's blowin' up so much wind
the bull's backwards an'
none of us knows which way is what,
An' him all twirly like a whirlin' dervish.

Them gypsy women say he got no earth,
can't get grounded
Sometimes I got to pull him down outta
the trees, him floatin' so high on
them lines of his –
What I'd give for a ploughman
or street sweeper, maybe –

All that hot wind blowin' the dust off me
leaves me bare and achin' for water, or ale, or
some of that
sweet wine from the tavern down the street
but all I got to wet me is the sound of my
twirly man, singing his love songs.

Winter Grass

Night stretches long
as if it knows
the words I long to say
are sealed inside

There must be a way
to tell you that when we first met,
spring visited
winter grass

And as light lifts the night
your spring rains
flood,
freeing these
thoughts of love

And Crazy, Too

She walks naked through the woods
where the sun darts through the leaves,
painting a diamond pattern on her breasts
baking them to well-done.

The deer and other wild creatures
don't seem to mind;
they watch as if they know,
then drop their eyes
they've no wish to intrude.

When the woods break and the meadow opens
she stretches out on a flat, gray rock
to let the wind tease
until she's as wild as they are.

And, crazy too, because
the very air
whispers his name —

Where the Wind Blows Wild

Where the wind blows wild
down by the sea
among cliffs undefiled
you trifled with me

The sun was high
and the white sand, hot
you whispered sweet lies
and oh, what they brought!

Now, the sun is low
the beach, sharp with shells
the wind blows cold
and my heart beats hollow
like the forlorn sound
   of a
      knelling
         bell

Like the Shoulder of a Child

Especially for Sarah

There comes a moment
like the soft slope
of a hill
when
summer is grown
her warm smiles and fertile mornings
evaporate
   into fall —
like the shoulder of a child
disappearing 'round a corner

and, in the winter
she'll be a woman.

Daughters and Mothers

Especially for Jo

Sometimes,
I take her doll
the soft one with the braided orange hair
    — and rock

the rocking makes a creaking
the way old attic boards will
when the wind tugs at them
    — it calms me

It calms me
the way most familiar things will,
and if I close my eyes
I can see her, over in the corner
    — playing
sucking on a strand of hair
and humming to herself

And I smile the way mothers will
even while my arms ache to hold her
    — like they never ached for a man

it's a woman thing, I guess
from daughter
    — to mother.

The Child Within

For Ariana with love

There is a child waking
within.
A sleepy-eyed child with tumbled curls
and that sleep-soft look
still on her face.
She takes me by the hand
leading me into the light,
almost dancing as she does,
Laughing
at the simplest things.

And she tells me
with her cherub's smile
that I really
must
get to know her

Sleepless Night

Deep in sleepless night I see her light
and I smile the way a mother will
though my arms ache to hold and stroke her, still
Those years are far gone
and memory separates then, from now
Yet still, I sit and rock
watching her at play

Night breaks and her light becomes day,
Brilliant day!
She waves farewell
then fades away.

Believing in Magic

If you were my little one, still
I'd tuck the down-filled comforter
up around your chin, all safe,
smooth your anxious forehead,
indulge a foolish grin.

I'd tell you stories of baby koalas,
Henny Penny and Peter Rabbit
I'd watch you dream your baby dreams,
and cradle your smile in my heart —

Believing in magic

But you're not mine, anymore
You're yours.
A soul in a world unknown.
And I share only what you offer —

Trying to believe in magic.

As I Am

For David

Lord,
You come to me like
the dawning of a slow morn.
Give me your light
That I may see your face.
Scatter your words,
lay them length to length
that I may understand,
You love me as I am.

Winter Solstice

The story of the Magnificat

Before I was born, I knew her.
She called me into being
with her singing.
    And so I was formed.

She sang of the Great One.
I grew warm where I slept,
and my embryonic dreams wrapped around me,
thick as lamb's wool,
    and clean as her lullabies.

Each night, when the hour grew deep,
My father would breathe soft words into our ear,
we were safe.
    waiting.

On Winter Solstice that year,
in the early hours before light, she sang again
"My soul magnifies the Lord,
and my spirit rejoices in God my Savior,
Holy, holy is God's name."

the place where I slept began to swell
I felt the Great One's hand upon me
in that moment, I wanted to be born,
to be delivered into her arms.

And so it was,
on the shortest day and longest night of the year,
I was born.

I shivered at the strange cool of the air.
They laid me against the supple warmth
of my mother's belly
where I tasted my father's tears.

Sinner's Tears

We could almost see
the heat rise
from their bodies
as she leaned into him
to loosen the leather
from his feet —
her fingers
had a common
street manner
yet,
they did not linger.

She dipped them
into a small brown bowl of warm oil
and myrrh
and began to smooth the stuff
into the rifts of his tired skin,
weeping wet, fat sinner's tears
as she worked —

Tears that collected the dust from his feet
and pooled on the floor
putting out
any possible fire
between them

Still, many of us frowned when she took her hair
and began to pass a tangle of it
between his toes
kissing his feet and ankles
as she moved

When she had finished
She gathered up her bowl, spices, and oils,
her long hair matted from the myrrh
tumbled down her back
and became lost in the blue folds
of her frock

She looked as if she wanted
to say something —
perhaps she did speak,
but one of us gave her a shove
and growled
"move on, woman, you embarrass us all"

But Jesus looked at us
one-by-one-by-one
eyes benign of judgment
and spoke yet again
in riddle or metaphor,
the meaning of which
we did not understand.

"Today," he said, "she has given me
all that she is."

That Man Jesus

A performance poem for live audience

Father,
it is I
Peter
the Rock
He called me that
and I tried to walk with him
before they crucified him,
but Father, that man Jesus, was always way ahead.

If I stopped to shake the hot sand from my feet
or draw a cool drink
why, it was a marathon just to catch up
you see, he was moving all the time
nomadic in thought and cause.
He could sleep in a storm at sea,
feed a swelling crowd on less than a boy would eat —
We didn't know what that man Jesus was all about

God,
if he had only explained himself,
let me know what to expect.
But he was always pulling surprises
and making headlines.
That man Jesus, he just didn't have any sense.
Imagine smearing mud on blind old Zephyrus
(we all knew a man born blind can't see)
and thinking he could keep it a secret!
Or the way he healed that woman on the Sabbath,
those Pharisees were furious!
It seemed foolish —
I was afraid.

And he confused me with his talk
of gaining the world
but giving up my soul —
I, a man whose hands are most comfortable

digging bait from the earth by the sea
and sweeping fish from the hemp of my nets.

Father,
that man Jesus
he tried to teach us things too simple
for our complicated minds.

during the climb to Calvary
I watched him, bent and sweating
and bleeding under the weight
of that massive cross,
the ugly crowd
excited by the smell of death —
his death
driving him forward.

I hid among them
ashamed that he knew me so well
as tears of denial bled against my face
like a rock in the rain

I must have gotten too close
I heard him groan —
saw him stumble.
He looked at me, then
the crowd nearly trampled me with their
deadly intent,
but I couldn't move
because in his eyes
I saw all the things I hadn't understood.

There was forgiveness
and more
I saw the souls of prophets past —
Abraham, David, Isaiah,
sitting in communion
with the souls of those yet unborn —
And I knew that we are all prophets
Sojourning souls.

Yesterday's headlines called him
common, a criminal, and a con man,
and people far into the future
will say his name as if it is a dirty curse.
But that day
long ago
at Calvary's cliff
my soul walked with him
and was reclaimed —
because that man Jesus
carried that cross
for me.

Bethlehem Night

Silence, silence in Bethlehem

There was a silence
in Bethlehem that night
where the babe lay asleep
Unlikely scene
The King in a place
so meager
lean

On that silent Bethlehem night.

Stars were strung in a chorus of light
The Son is born, there is peace tonight.

de Profundus
(Out of the Depths)

Out of the deep I cry
Lord!
I am alone, dry
dust and bone I wander
wondering
if I die
who will know?

        Into the deep I stumble
        Lord!
        I am weak, I crumble
        knowing into sin
        I tumble
        and Lord
        who will know?

                Into the deep, you came
                Lord!
                Is it you calling my name?
                Give me your hand,
                ease my pain
                Here in the deep, Lord
                You know.

Confessions of the Twelfth Man

I felt the stubble of his beard
drag across my lips
as I kissed him
and my eyes sought his
by accident

Oh, I tried not to look
but the night was deep
with betrayal —

The earth growled
and the taut garden air
blotted out the white, clean smell
of the lilies

But those eyes —
His eyes
saw everything —
knew everything

And as the soldiers led him away
the dirty silver pieces they tossed at my feet
began to bleed in the sand

And I, just a pawn in the plan

Holy Spirit, Come

Holy Spirit, come!
On the wing of mystic flight
breathe your will, be my light
give my heart your truth to hold
and I will speak it, clear and bold.
When at dawn the angels gather
all I've left undone won't matter
I shall close my eyes in sleep
and dwell in His eternal peace.
earthly spirit, spun;
Holy Spirit come!

www.ingramcontent.com/pod-product-compliance
Lightning Source LLC
LaVergne TN
LVHW022112080426
835511LV00007B/767